An Internal Audit

by

Mette Marx

Dedicated to my Abba Father,

Who knows me as I am,

And loves me enough

To lead me along the path called

Change.

There are always a multitude of people that need to be acknowledged and thanked concerning a project such as this one. Space does not allow me to list everyone; however, there are these that I *must* say thank you to:

First and foremost, to my husband Richard. For all of the days of frozen burritos and frozen pizza, for your seemingly unending patience, I thank you. None of this would be possible without you.

To Kathy Hamlett, friend, sister, and Torah teacher extraordinaire. Thank you for not only keeping me on my Torah path, but also doctrinally correct.

To Rabbi Steve Berkson, thank you. I listen more than you think I do!

To Dillard and Reva Griffin. The two of you are a tremendous example to me, of what a Torah-observant couple should *be*. I appreciate you both, and I appreciate your prayers.

And to my editor, Tammy Souch. Our getting together was by *divine appointment*—I am convinced. Without you, this book would not be what it is. Thank you, dear lady!

INTRODUCTION

According to the Rabbinic, civil calendar, the month of Elul is the last month of the year, immediately followed by the fall High Holy Days of Rosh Hashanah, Yom Kippur, and the Feast of Sukkot. That being said, the month of Elul is steeped in history and tradition, of which most is good, and well worth observing. Jewish wisdom believes that on the 1st of Elul, Moses re-ascended the mountain of Elohim, to not only receive the second set of tablets, but also the assurance of forgiveness for the sin of the Golden Calf. Moses was again on this mountain for another forty days, not descending until the 10th of Tishri, the Day of Atonement, Yom Kippur.

These intense forty days from the 1st of Elul until the 10th of Tishri are also known as *Yemei Ratzon*, the Days of Favor, since it was during this time that the nation of Israel found favor with Elohim, and the sin of the Golden Calf was finally forgiven[1]. Many ancient Jewish sages also believed that this is the time when the "King is in the field," meaning that our King of Kings is more accessible during this time of favor, reaching out to us with forgiveness.[2] This time period is also called the "Season of Teshuvah," a time to repent, turn away from that which has led us astray, make confession to our Creator, seek forgiveness, and, if necessary, make restitution to those we have wronged.[3] In Aramaic, the word Elul means "to search," which is what we are doing: opening ourselves up to the searchlight of the Spirit of YHWH, as the cleansing process begins, from the inside out.

This book is a collection of forty essays, one for each day of this Season of Teshuvah. If judgment begins with the house of Elohim, then the cleansing process must first begin with us, those of us who belong to *Him*, the God of Abraham, Isaac, and Jacob (see 1Pet 4:17). A word of warning, however: this book is not for everyone. These essays are not written in my normal style of encouragement and edification; they are not sugar-coated in any way. Each one is written with the challenge to change, change for the better, to become

---

[1] http://hebrew4christians.com/Holidays/Fall_Holidays/Elul/elul.html
[2] http://www.chabad.org/theJewishWoman/article_cdo/aid/424441/jewish/
The-Jewish-Heart.htm
[3] http://hebrew4christians.com/Holidays/Fall_Holidays/Elul/elul.html

more conformed to the image of Messiah Yeshua within us. There will be many that will begin this process, only to quit after a certain amount of time; the reason being that this process of change will become too hard, too personal. As the old saying goes, "no sweat, no gain."

Again, this book is put together similar to the Yom Berekha book, in that there is room for daily journaling, something I encourage each of you to do. And, as the dates of Elul 1 to Tishri 10 are the same year after year, so too this book may be used for many years in the future, as a yearly reminder, so to speak, of how far we have come. May we all press forward to the goal of becoming the type of person that a King would want to spend eternity with. Amein.

"Seek יהוה [YHWH] while He is to be found, call on Him while He is near. Let the wrong forsake his way, and the unrighteous man his thoughts. Let him return to יהוה, [YHWH] who has compassion on him, and to our Elohim, for He pardons much." (Isa 55:6-7)

Elul 1

Examine Yourself

"For if we were to EXAMINE OURSELVES, we would not be judged." (1Cor 11:31, emphasis mine)

We *know* when we have deliberately done something wrong, something we should not have done. It is unfortunate that too often we choose to ignore the voice of our conscience, and disregard the wrongdoing we have done. The *Ruach HaKodesh*, Spirit of YHWH, will convict us of what is right and truth; this is one of the functions of the Set-Apart Spirit (see John 16:8, 13 Amplified Bible, Classic Edition). It is, however, *our own* responsibility to test and examine *ourselves*. Nowhere in the Word of Elohim is there such a thing as a "Ministry of Critique," where we are called upon to examine anyone *other* than ourselves. We are to look at our *own* lives (no one else's), hold them up and compare them to the standard that is found within the pages of the *Word*, the Torah. We are also to look closely at the life of Messiah Yeshua, the *living* Word, for He is our example in all things.

Am I truthfully lacking in some areas? Am I successfully 'walking the talk'? Has the Spirit of YHWH pointed out, through His Word, areas in my character and personality that need adjusting? Is my lifestyle not, perhaps, giving honor to my Elohim as much as it could? And should?

It is at *this* point where we will find it necessary to yield and surrender. When we stop, and submit to our Master Yeshua in those rotten and corrupted areas of our lives, we have successfully examined and judged ourselves. We then do *teshuva*, repent, and invite *Him* to perfect those things that concern us (see Ps 138:8).

Discipleship and discipline walk hand in hand. I cannot claim to be a disciple of YHWH Elohim *if* I am not willing to live a disciplined life of self-examination and scrutiny. It is such a simple thing to ask the Spirit of YHWH to shine a light of illumination on any area of our lives that is not pleasing to our Creator, and then invite Him to help us change what needs to be changed. Is this not what we desire: to become that person our Elohim desires to spend eternity with?

For these next 40 days, leading up to Yom Kippur (the Day of Atonement), it is my hope that we can spend some time turning the spotlight inward, in examining ourselves, and doing some serious housecleaning. Through it all, let us determine to come up to the next level, clean the crud off of the glass, and reflect more of the light and love of our Creator. Amein...

Notes:

_____

_____

_____

_____

_____

_____

_____

_____

_____

_____

_____

_____

_____

_____

_____

_____

_____

_____

_____

_____

_____

Elul 2

Clanging Noise

"If I speak with the tongues of men and of messengers, but DO NOT HAVE LOVE, I have become as sounding brass or a clanging cymbal." (1Cor 13:1, emphasis mine)

Our Creator is not against us learning new and multiple languages. It is a necessary skill if we are to communicate the *Good News* of Messiah Yeshua, and the truth of Torah, to a lost and dying world. What our Elohim *is* against is the attitude with which it is done—if it is "me, myself, and I" speaking in the different tongues, and glorifying myself in the doing. Our gifts and talents are given to us by our Elohim; they are to bring glory to *Him*, and not to us. Any righteousness we have is because of our obedience to Torah, because of our relationship with Messiah Yeshua, and because *He* is our righteousness (see 1Cor 1:30).

When we speak from the platform of self-exaltation, it is always off-key, and never harmonious. Most of us can take a moment and think of at least one person that enjoys hearing *themselves* speak—we can be generous, and call this being long-winded. The subject material of such a one is most generally of themselves, and of their exploits.

What do *I* sound like, Abba, when I speak? Am I just making a lot of noise promoting myself, a brass band totally out of harmony? Am I a 'clanging noise'? Or does my speech reflect the love of Messiah Yeshua, and my commitment to Him who gave His life for me? Is there someone that I have offended with words that I spoke, someone to whom I need to be restored to?

Abba, *Abba*, set a guard over my tongue. Help me to say only those things that will bring *You* honor and glory, words of *life*. Let everything that comes out of my mouth be well-seasoned with the love of Elohim, sprinkled with Your grace, watered with the Rivers of Living Water, and gently tended by the Heavenly Gardener. In the Name of my Messiah, Yeshua of Nazareth, I pray. Amein.

"Therefore, as chosen ones of Elohim, set-apart and beloved, PUT ON compassion, kindness, humbleness of mind, meekness, patience, BEARING WITH one another, and FORGIVING each other if anyone has a complaint against another, indeed, as Messiah forgave you so also should you. But above all these PUT ON LOVE, which is a bond of the perfection." (Col 3:12-14, emphasis mine)

Notes:

_____

_____

_____

_____

_____

_____

_____

_____

_____

_____

_____

_____

_____

_____

_____

_____

_____

_____

_____

_____

_____

Elul 3

Motives

"And if I have prophecy, and know all secrets and all knowledge, and if I have all belief, so as to remove mountains, but do not have love, I am none at all." (1Cor 13:2)

There is a story, found in Numbers 22-24, of a man supposedly having prophetic powers (as what is spoken of in our opening verse), yet finding it impossible to curse YHWH's people. Balaam tried; he had the promise of great wealth and reputation held out to him as a reward, but he could not curse what YHWH had commanded him to bless. Needless to say, his motive was in the wrong ballpark.

Centuries ago, the Greek people were a nation famous for their great speaking skills and intellect. In today's language, they would have been called "smooth talkers." But it was all natural, human knowledge and talent, of which they were very proud. For the most part, there was little, or no love, for our YHWH Elohim in them. Today, many colleges and universities teach classes on public speaking and presentation, and these classes in themselves are not wrong or bad. But as it was in the time of the ancient Greeks, the whole concept of public speaking today has little to do with the love of our Abba Father, and His Son Yeshua. Many of those that engage in this activity do so from the need of self-exaltation.

For those of us that claim to be children of the God of Abraham, Isaac, and Jacob, it is to us the Rav Sha'ul, the Apostle Paul, is addressing his remarks in our opening verse. He is very specific concerning our motives and attitudes in the public forum. If we do not have YAH's love reflecting *in* and *through* us, we are *nothing*... It is a question I ask myself continually, in what I write: who does this glorify and bring honor to? What is *my* motive for doing what I do? May it always point to YHWH my Elohim, who gives me the words to write.

"Search me, O Ěl, and know my heart; Try me, and know my thoughts; And see if an idolatrous way is in me, And lead me in the way everlasting." (Ps 139:23-24)

Notes:

_____

_____

_____

_____

_____

_____

_____

_____

_____

_____

_____

_____

_____

_____

_____

_____

_____

_____

_____

_____

_____

_____

_____

_____

Elul 4

Alms

"Even if I dole out all that I have [to the poor in providing] food, and if I surrender my body to be burned OR IN ORDER THAT I MAY GLORY, but have not love (God's love in me), I gain nothing." (1Cor 13:3 AMPC, emphasis mine)

Messiah Yeshua gave us specific instructions concerning *how* we are to pursue our charitable deeds: they were to be done quietly, even secretly, without drawing undue attention to ourselves (see Mat 6:1-4). Anything else is labeled hypocritical and "play-acting," not worthy of recognition, or much of a reward. When we seek to gain recognition, acceptance, and love through our good works and actions, we have perverted what YHWH created us for. We have doomed ourselves to eventual failure.

YHWH our Elohim created us *needing* to be loved, needing to be accepted, and needing to be needed. However, those needs are to be met *first* in and through Him, *then* in each other, and not in any other way. Too often we get things backward, try to find love in being recognized, and for all the wrong reasons. Most often this recognition will end up in an ego-trip, self-exaltation, and self-love, which is *not* God's way.

The Word of God teaches us that there is not one good thing that dwells within us (Rom 7:18), and that our hearts are both deceitful and wicked, and cannot be trusted (Jer 17:9). It is only because of YHWH's love that has been poured *in* our hearts by the His Spirit (who was given to us) that we even begin to understand what the love of our Elohim is all about (Rom 5:5). And one of the first things that we learn is that it is *not* about us; it is *all* about Him.

Am I striving to draw subtle attention to myself in my act of giving? Do I have ulterior motives when I choose to give? Do I truly give without expecting anything in return, or am I continuously waiting to be reciprocated? Is there one to whom I *should* have given, but did not, and do I now need to ask forgiveness of that person?

Father, forgive me for my wrong motives in my giving—if only I would learn to not let the right hand know what the left hand is doing! Teach me to be self-less, and Messiah-like, that the image of Messiah Yeshua would be reflected in and through me to the world around me. Teach me to give, not of obligation, but because of the love You have poured out upon me. In the Name that is above every name, Yeshua of Nazareth, I pray! Amein...

"For Elohim so LOVED THE WORLD that He gave His only brought-forth Son, so that everyone who believes in Him should not perish but possess everlasting life." (John 3:16, emphasis mine)

Notes:

_____

_____

_____

_____

_____

_____

_____

_____

_____

_____

_____

_____

_____

_____

_____

_____

_____

_____

_____

_____

_____

Elul 5

Endures Long

"Love ENDURES long ... " (1Cor 13:4 AMPC, emphasis mine)

Noah Webster defines "endure" as "to last; to remain; TO BEAR WITH PATIENCE; to suffer without resistance, or without yielding; to bear without sinking under pressure."[4] It seems a contradictory picture to imagine love as "bearing up without sinking under pressure," or "suffering without resistance," but I believe the perfect example of this type of love is found in the life of Messiah Yeshua, while He walked through the short time span of His three-and-a-half-year ministry.

Only because of the love that our Messiah had for the Father, and the love that the Father had for His Son, was Yeshua able to endure all that He went through on the way to the stake. Yeshua was able to look *beyond* the cross, and see the result of His love: *our redemption*. Regardless of how He was treated, regardless of what was said to Him, *about* Him, because of Him, He kept His eyes on *what* He was purchasing, and *knew* that it was all worth it (Heb 12:2).

We now have this same love abiding within us (Rom 5:5), should we choose to recognize and acknowledge it. As He was, so are we to be (1John 4:17); as Yeshua loved, so are we to love.

Am I willing to love and "endure long," regardless of what circumstances and situations come my way? Am I able to "bear with patience" the trials and tribulations that are part and parcel of everyday life? Do I sink when pressure is applied to my relationships with others? Have I given up too quickly on a relationship with a certain one, and is there someone that I now need to be restored to?

---

[4] American Dictionary of the English Language, Noah Webster, 1828, emphasis mine

Abba, teach me, teach *me* to love as *You* love, with the everlasting love that knows no end. Only as I learn to love others as *You* love, will the world know that Messiah Yeshua truly is LORD over all the earth, that *Your* kingdom has come, and that *Your* will is done, on earth as it is in heaven. In the Name that is above every name I pray, Yeshua our Messiah, Amein.

"This is my command: that you KEEP ON loving each other just as I have loved you." (John 15:12 CJB, emphasis mine)

"For the entire Torah is completed in one word, in this, 'You shall love your neighbour as yourself.'" (Gal 5:14)

Notes:

_____

_____

_____

_____

_____

_____

_____

_____

_____

_____

_____

_____

_____

_____

_____

_____

_____

_____

_____

_____

Elul 6

Patient and Kind

"Love ... is patient AND kind ... " (1Cor 13:4 AMPC, emphasis mine)

In the ninth chapter of Luke, we find Messiah Yeshua reprimanding His disciples (Luke 9:51-56). All power and authority had been given to them (Luke 9:1). However, their desire was to abuse this *holy* authority and power. Impatient and highly offended with the rejection that had been given them by a particular Samaritan town, the disciples wanted to call fire down from heaven, destroy the town, *and* everyone in it.

People who are impatient in their nature are, as a rule, selfish and self-centered. They are on their own agenda, and have little time for the needs, wants, and desires of others, unless they should coincide with their own. Their love is turned *inward*, toward themselves, and they naturally expect, and will even demand, everyone to be patient and kind with *them*. There is even a subtle form of pride found in impatience; it surfaces with an attitude of "out of my way, I can do this faster (and better) than you can." This type of person will never look beyond themselves to *see* a need other than their own, to *see* the hurt that should be healed, and the pain that requires comforting.

Have I been impatient and short with others? Have I been unkind in my thoughts, words, and actions? Have I failed to extend the hand that was needed? Have I demanded what I was not willing to give? Have I been so wrapped up in myself, that I have deliberately blinded myself to those around me? Is there one that I now need to seek forgiveness from, one that I was unkind toward?

When YHWH's love fills our hearts, the fruits of His Set-Apart Spirit (such as the fruits of patience and kindness—see Gal 5:22), will begin to blossom. It will pour out of us toward others, because YAH's love gives, gives, gives. We give patience and kindness by simply reflecting the same patience that our Master has had with us, in all of our missteps, stumblings, and failures. We hold our hand out to our brother/sister, and say, "Here, let me help you. I have walked this particular path, and I know where the stones are. See my knees? I fell often..."

"And BE KIND towards one another, tenderhearted, forgiving one another, as Elohim also forgave you in Messiah." (Eph 4:32, emphasis mine)

"I call upon you therefore, I the prisoner of the Master, to walk worthily of the calling with which you were called, with all humility and meekness, with patience, bearing with one another in love, being eager to guard the unity of the Spirit in the bond of peace ..." (Eph 4:1-3)

Notes:

_____

_____

_____

_____

_____

_____

_____

_____

_____

_____

_____

_____

_____

_____

_____

_____

_____

_____

_____

Elul 7

Servant's Heart

"Love NEVER is envious nor boils over with jealousy ..." (1Cor 13:4 AMPC, emphasis mine)

The ancient sages believe that when our Elohim first "formed" (*yâtsar,* Strong's H3335, see Gen 2:7) man, it was with two conflicting inclinations and impulses: one positive, or good (*yetzer hatov*); and one negative, or bad (*yetzer hara*). It is always our free will and choice which inclination we choose to listen and submit to, by choosing life, and doing what is right (Torah), or by choosing death, and doing what is evil and wrong (Deu 30:19). Truthfully, the adversary has little to do with the choices we make. *We* decide what nature we will follow.

Jealousy and envy are the offspring of pride, which has its origin in our *yetzer hara,* our evil inclination. Noah Webster defines "pride" as "inordinate self-esteem; an unreasonable conceit of one's own superiority in talents, beauty, wealth, accomplishments, rank or elevation in office, which manifests itself in lofty airs, distance, reserve, and often in contempt of others."[5] When I allow myself to walk in this form of the evil inclination, I will always be resentful and coveting of the gifts, talents, and possessions of others.

How am I to deal with all of this? Am I living my life in envy and jealousy toward others? Do I deliberately resent those who are more gifted, talented, have more...? Is there someone that I have been jealous of and resented that I now need to ask forgiveness from?

How do I correct this mentally? I *must* die daily, to *all* the works of the flesh, and the *yetzer hara,* as it attempts to rise up and dominate me (see Rom 7 and 8). I *must* submit to the working of the *Ruach HaKodesh,* the HOLY Spirit, and

---

[5] ibid

allow the Fruit of the Spirit of truth to mature in my life (see Gal 5:16-26, especially from the Amplified Bible). And I must see myself as I truly am: a servant of *El Elyon,* the *Most high* Elohim.

Servants, bondservants, and slaves have little time to be envious or jealous, especially if we are servants by *choice.* A servant is one who serves, and our Messiah Yeshua says of Himself, that *He* came to serve (Mark 10:45). Should I not also do the same? The heart of the servant is the *willingness* to serve, at *all* times, at *all* costs, without thought to themselves. I serve, first because I love *Him* who died for me, and second, because *He* is my example in one who comes to serve.

"For you, brethren, were [indeed] called to freedom; only [do not let your] freedom be an incentive to your flesh and an opportunity or excuse [for selfishness], but THROUGH LOVE YOU SHOULD SERVE ONE ANOTHER." (Gal 5:13 AMPC, emphasis mine)

Notes:

_____

_____

_____

_____

_____

_____

_____

_____

_____

_____

_____

_____

_____

_____

_____

Elul 8

Boasting

"Love ... is not boastful or vainglorious ... " (1Cor 13:4 AMPC)

Noah Webster defines boast as "to brag; to make a VAIN DISPLAY, in speech, of one's own worth, property, or actions; to glory; to exalt one's self; to speak of with pride, vanity or exultation, with a view to SELF-COMMENDATION (praise); expression of pride."[6] Boasting is another offspring of pride and vanity, which serves the god of *I*—self-centeredness, self-worship, self-exaltation.

The Word of Elohim tells us that our Creator will share His glory with *no one* (Isa 42:8; 48:11); we need to meditate on why. There is no selfishness or vanity *in* Him; on the contrary. Our Abba Father is a kind and generous parent, giving, caring, with our best interests always before Him. He understands that the very moment we take our eyes *off* of Him, focus them on our own achievements, our*selves*, we will begin to worship our*selves*. This is the first step toward self-destruction. Our Creator did not create us for us to destroy ourselves. We were created to enjoy fellowship with *Him*.

Of *whom* do I boast? Of *what* do I boast? If it has anything to do with me, or my own achievements, my own possessions, there is a serpent in the garden ("you will be like Elohim ... " see Gen 3:5). What, therefore, *do* I boast about? I brag about my Elohim. I boast about His goodness, His faithfulness, His love, His virtue, His character, how wonderful He is to *me*, His child.

Are these things not worth boasting about? Don't you enjoy it when you hear *your* children saying, "My Mommy/Daddy is the *best* in the w-h-o-l-e wide world!" And won't you stop everything you are doing just to go love on that child? Isn't it possible our heavenly Father might feel the same way?

---

[6] ibid

"Thus said יהוה [YHWH], "Let not the wise boast in his wisdom, let not the mighty boast in his might, nor let the rich boast in his riches, but let him who boasts boast of this, that he UNDERSTANDS AND KNOWS ME, that I am יהוה [YHWH], doing kindness, right-ruling, and righteousness in the earth. For in these I delight," declares יהוה [YHWH]." (Jer 9:23-24, emphasis mine)

"My being makes its boast in יהוה [YHWH]; Let the humble hear and be glad." (Ps 34:2)

Notes:

_____

_____

_____

_____

_____

_____

_____

_____

_____

_____

_____

_____

_____

_____

_____

_____

_____

_____

_____

_____

_____

Elul 9

On Display

"Love ... does not display itself haughtily." (1Cor 13:4 AMPC)

My husband, as a young boy, was fortunate enough to visit and tour the Smithsonian Institute in Washington, D. C.; it was an experience that he has never forgotten. Whether your interest is science, history, or nature, there are many, many exhibits and displays to capture and hold your attention. Every display is brilliantly designed, executed, and maintained, created with one purpose in mind: to delight its audience.

Noah Webster, in his dictionary of 1828, defines "display" as "literally, to unfold; hence, to open; to spread wide; to expand; to show; to exhibit to the eyes or to the mind; to make manifest"[7]. "Haughtily," as found in our opening verse, is another word for "arrogantly"[8]—the very opposite of a humble and contrite spirit (Isa 57:15). Therefore, what our Elohim is telling us here is that *His* love (that is shed abroad in our hearts by His *Ruach*, His Spirit, Rom 5:5) will *never* display itself, exhibit itself, manifest itself in a proud, arrogant, self-centered, or conceited manner.

We, as children of the Elohim of Abraham, Isaac, and Jacob, are *all* on display, but it is our choice as to how we *act* while on display. No, we are not perfect, and yes, we stumble and fall, but in our imperfections and failures, we understand the concept of *teshuvah* (true, heart-felt repentance), running *to* our Father, receiving the forgiveness and healing needed.

All of this has everything to do with our "heart attitude" while the world watches us. Am I like the Pharisee, reminding YHWH of how righteous I am, of how good I am, of how holy and set-apart I am, all the while "struttin' my

---

[7] Ibid
[8] http://www.thesaurus.com/browse/haughtily?s=t

stuff," and making sure everyone sees it (Luke 18:10-12)? Or am I like the tax collector, humble, not even willing to raise my eyes heavenward, asking only for mercy (Luke 18:13)? And let me present to you one more scenario: what am I like when *no one* is watching? This is when *He* is watching—the Omnipotent, Omniscient, Omnipresent Creator of us all, our Messiah, Redeemer, and soon-coming King.

Our lives are to be an epistle of Yeshua, known and read by all men (2Cor 3:2-3). What is my epistle saying to you? What is your epistle saying to me?

YHWH Elohim, I come to You, thanking You that You dwell with the one that is of a humble and broken spirit. Father, while I walk this world as Your ambassador, let me be ever conscious of *whose* light is to shine brightly. Let it shine clearly, that all would know that I am Your child, that I belong to You. Help me to not hinder the love of my Creator from flowing through me to others; let me be the channel that *you* desire me to be. In the Name of Messiah Yeshua, I pray. Amein.

"For I resolved not to know any matter among you except יהושע [Yeshua] Messiah and Him impaled." (1Cor 2:2)

Notes:

_____

_____

_____

_____

_____

_____

_____

_____

_____

_____

_____

_____

_____

Elul 10

Humility

"{Love} ... is not conceited (arrogant and INFLATED WITH PRIDE); it is not rude (unmannerly) and does not act unbecomingly." (1Cor 13:5 AMPC, emphasis and insert mine)

Some years ago, there was a meeting of hot air balloon enthusiasts in Southwestern Wyoming. It was breath-taking to watch the vivid and colorful display of these majestic balloons as they moved across the horizon. Abba Father used this opportunity, and the images of the hot air balloons, to teach me about being "inflated with pride." When I am "full of hot air," I am very much like one of these big balloons, rising with self-importance, and being carried along with the wind of pride. And in a similar fashion, pride can also be ill mannered, with little or no consideration for others, and like these big balloons when the wind begins to get rough, there is virtually no controlling it.

On the flip side of the coin, humility is the opposite of all arrogance, pride, and conceit, and basically means a freedom from all of the above. We must be aware of the fact that if it were not for Messiah Yeshua, we are of ourselves of little or no worth. It is His life *in us* that makes us worthy, and *because* we acknowledge and recognize this, we can joyfully walk in submission to His Torah, *His* will for our lives. Only as we travel the path called "yielded," in *true* humility, can we be the siphon that His love will flow through.

Am I conceited, puffed up with my own self-importance? Am I rude, both in the words that I use, and the actions that I take? What of my manners? Do they reflect to Whom I belong? Are my actions an embarrassment to my Father? Have I been rude to someone in the past, someone that I now need to go and ask forgiveness from?

"A man's pride will bring him low, but he who is of a humble spirit will obtain honor." (Pro 29:23 AMPC)

"Because of this He says, 'Elohim resists the proud, but gives favour to the humble.'" (Jam 4:6)

"A man can counterfeit love, he can counterfeit faith, he can counterfeit hope and all the other graces, but it is VERY DIFFICULT to counterfeit humility." (emphasis mine)

DWIGHT LYMAN MOODY (1837–1899)

Notes:

_____

_____

_____

_____

_____

_____

_____

_____

_____

_____

_____

_____

_____

_____

_____

_____

_____

_____

_____

_____

_____

Elul 11

Not My Own

"Love (God's love in us) does not insist on its own rights or its own way, for it is not self-seeking ... " (1Cor 13:5 AMPC)

Our United States Constitution, including the Bill of Rights, was written—based upon biblical principles—to protect our individual rights from tyrannical and dictatorial control. There are many that would say that our present government is trying to legislate these rights away from us; I am not attempting to discuss or debate this issue. However, because of these times that we live in, there are those who have developed the mind-set of "I have *my* rights," which, in itself, has an element of truth to it.

Does it really? If we confess Messiah Yeshua as our Master and Redeemer, then we have been bought with a price, a very costly price: that price being *His* life and *His* blood, which He bled out for each one of us. If He was willing to give up all of His rights as the Son of the Living Elohim (Phi 2:7; 2Cor 8:9), should we not do the same? The Word of our Creator tells us that our lives are no longer our own, to do with as *we* please, which basically means, we no longer belong to ourselves (1Cor 6:19-20).

Time to look inward: am I self-seeking? Do I always insist on having my own way, on doing everything *my* way? Do I continually insist others adhere to what I see as "*my* rights"—even if they might conflict with the dictates of Torah? Have I placed what is mine and my rights above that of my neighbor?

If we are to live out our lives as an extension of *Him*, our Messiah King, then we must also radiate His love in and through us to the world around us, by *not* insisting on our *own* way, our *own* rights, just as *He* never did (Mat 20:28; 26:42).

"And let us not lose heart in doing good, for in due season we shall reap if we do not grow weary. So then, as we have occasion, let us do good to all, especially to those who are of the household of the belief." (Gal 6:9-10)

"Love each other devotedly and with brotherly love; and SET EXAMPLES FOR EACH OTHER in showing respect." (Rom 12:10 CJB, emphasis mine)

Notes:

_____

_____

_____

_____

_____

_____

_____

_____

_____

_____

_____

_____

_____

_____

_____

_____

_____

_____

_____

_____

_____

_____

Elul 12

Touchy

"{Love} ... is not TOUCHY or FRETFUL or RESENTFUL ..." (1Cor 13:5 AMPC, insert and emphasis mine)

Let us take a further look at these three words found in the above verse. Noah Webster defines "touchy" as "peevish; irritable; irascible [easily provoked]; apt to take fire." "Fretful" is defined as "disposed to fret; ill-humored; peevish; angry; in a state of vexation." And the word "resentful" is defined as "easily provoked to anger; of an irritable temper."[9] All three of these words represent *symptoms* found in individuals who have been offended, and very possibly live with bitterness and unforgiveness as constant companions.

Messiah Yeshua warned us that offenses would come (Luke 17:1), but in the verses following this warning, His instructions were specific concerning forgiveness (Luke 17:3-4). Yet how do we recognize offenses? How do we know when we are offended? May I ask you this: who are you irritated at? Who has hurt your feelings lately? Who do you hold a grudge against? Who has said something to you that has completely "ticked you off"? If you have *not* forgiven what has been done/said to you—if you have *not* released it to the Father—and prayed blessings over the individual(s), if you are still nursing and rehearsing a certain incident, then it is more than likely you have been offended, and are struggling with unforgiveness.

We cannot pretend to be disciples of YHWH our Elohim, and be offended at like-minded brothers and sisters, those sharing the same beliefs in the God of Abraham, Isaac, and Jacob—to do so is hypocritical. If we are born-again of the incorruptible seed of *Elohim Chayim*, the Living God (1Pet 1:23; Deu 5:26), then God's love for us has already been poured out in our hearts through the *Ruach HaKodesh* (Rom 5:5). The same power that raised Yeshua from the dead,

---

[9] American Dictionary of the English Language, Noah Webster, 1828

and called Lazarus forth from the tomb, is *in* us, to assist us in walking in love and forgiveness, as the living epistles (2Cor 3:2-3) that our Master asks us to be.

Love covers. Love not only forgets, but it buries the axe handle too, so that it can never be dug back up again. In the story related to us of Noah, when in his drunkenness, he lay exposed, two of his three sons walked backward holding a covering with which to cover him, so as not to look upon his nakedness (Gen 9:23). Love covers. Always.

"And above all have fervent love for one another, because love covers a great number of sins." (1Pet 4:8)

"He who conceals an offense promotes love, but he who harps on it can separate even close friends." (Pro 17:9 CJB)

Notes:

_____

_____

_____

_____

_____

_____

_____

_____

_____

_____

_____

_____

_____

_____

_____

_____

Elul 13

No Account

"{Love} ... *takes no account of the evil done to it [it pays no attention to a suffered wrong].*" (1Cor 13:5 AMPC, insert mine)

There is told to us a story in the Tanakh—the Old Testament—of how ten brothers, jealous of the youngest one, sold this younger brother into slavery, never expecting to see him again (Gen 37:12-36). Elohim, however, had other plans, and worked all things together for the good of everyone concerned (Rom 8:28). Our Creator used these very circumstances for the deliverance of the entire family, teaching a significant lesson to all of us through the ages. This younger brother, Joseph, rose from the status of a lowly slave in a prison, to that of prime minister of *all* of Egypt, never holding a grudge against his brothers for what they did to him (Gen 45:5-9; 50:19-20). Joseph's trust was in his Elohim, knowing that God was with him, and would turn all things around for good (Gen 39:2-3, 21,23; 41:38).

I have asked myself if I should ever find myself in a similar situation, and in the same "shoes," would I be so generous and forgiving? If there were someone attempting to take my life, or attempting to sell me into slavery—or bring harm to my loved ones—would I take "no account of the evil"? We know that it *is* possible to be that way, for we have Joseph as one example, and Messiah Yeshua as another. Yeshua Himself tells us to "love your enemies; bless those cursing you, do good to those hating you, and pray for those insulting and persecuting you, so that you become sons of your Father in the heavens" (Mat 5:44-45).

Those of us that live in the United States have been blessed with a freedom that many in the world do not have, and very often we take this freedom for granted. But as the days before our Messiah King's return grow increasingly shorter, we too may suffer persecution for the stand that we choose to take in *His Name*, Yeshua HaMashiach. Will we take "no account" of the wrong done to us? Will we continue to walk in the love and forgiveness of our Master, toward those that come against us, because of *Whom* we belong to?

"Beloved ones, let us love one another, because love is of Elohim, and everyone who loves has been born of Elohim, and knows Elohim." (1John 4:7)

"Don't let love be a mere outward show. Recoil from what is evil, and cling to what is good. Love each other devotedly and with brotherly love; and set examples for each other in showing respect ... Bless those who persecute you — bless them, don't curse them!" (Rom 12:9-10,14 CJB)

Notes:

_____

_____

_____

_____

_____

_____

_____

_____

_____

_____

_____

_____

_____

_____

_____

_____

_____

_____

_____

_____

Elul 14

When Truth Prevails

"{LOVE} ... does not rejoice at injustice and unrighteousness, but rejoices when right and truth prevail." (1 Cor 13:6 AMPC, insert mine)

Do I rejoice—am I glad—when that which is right and true triumphs, even when it is not necessarily to my benefit? Or do I flippantly and casually acknowledge that yes, right has prevailed against that which is wrong, but I do not rejoice in it?

The Book of Esther relates to us the story of the near annihilation of the Jewish people, brought about by one man: Haman, a descendant of Agag, the Amalekite king who indirectly began the downward spiral that resulted in King Saul's loss of the throne of Israel (see 1Sam 15). Because of this, Haman's hatred for the man Mordecai, and for *all* the Jewish people, he plots to have all of the Jews killed. Queen Esther calls upon her Jewish brethren to join her in a time of fasting and prayer, after which she approaches King Ahasuerus to reveal Haman's wicked plot. The tables turn on Haman, and righteousness and truth prevail (Est 7).

Truth and righteousness begin with our *El Emet*, the God of truth (John 1:17, Ps 31:5, Ps 33:5). Because Messiah Yeshua is *"the way, the truth, and the life"* (John 14:6, emphasis mine), truth means victory, when we walk in *His* truth. And because Yeshua is the Living Word (John 1:1), we also know that His Word is truth, absolute truth (see John 17:17, Ps 119:142).

Throughout the Word of our Elohim, we find mention of several things that are said to "endure forever": the throne of YHWH (Lam 5:19), the Kingdom of YHWH (Dan 4:34), the faithfulness of YHWH (Ps 117:2), the works of Adonai Elohim (Ecc 3:14), the Name of YHWH (Ps 135:13), the *Word* of our God (1Pet 1:25), and the love of our Abba Father (1Chr 16:34, Ps 100:5). This is certainly not a complete list. However, when we consider the righteousness of YHWH, there should never be any question as to it enduring forever, because righteous is

Who and *What* He is.

"His work is honorable and glorious; and His righteousness is standing FOREVER." Ps 111:3 HRB, emphasis mine)

Notes:

_____

_____

_____

_____

_____

_____

_____

_____

_____

_____

_____

_____

_____

_____

_____

_____

_____

_____

_____

_____

_____

_____

Elul 15

Bearing Up

"Love bears up under anything and everything that comes ... " (1Cor 13:7 AMPC)

It is an acknowledged fact that Rav Sha'ul (the Apostle Paul), a *Jewish* Pharisee (see Acts 21:39, 23:6), was responsible for writing more than half of the *Brit Chadashah* (New Testament). Sha'ul considered himself the "Apostle to the Gentiles" (Rom 11:13), and it is through his commitment to this calling that the Word of YHWH was taught to those not of the "nation" of Israel.

The Rabbi's road was not an easy one, and it is possible our Master revealed to him, in part, that it would be difficult. Sha'ul lists for us some of the physical hardships that he went through in 2Cor 11:23-27, a list I am sure that none of us would want to participate in. And yet, his greatest concern was for the flock that YHWH had entrusted to his care (see 2Cor 11:28-29)!

The last years of the Rabbi's life were spent in an underground prison cell, part of the myriad of caves and tunnels beneath the city of Rome, many times saturated with the raw sewage that flowed through these tunnels. It was from this cell that some of his epistles were written, while he was awaiting his execution at the hands of the worst emperor that Rome had ever known. Truly, this amazing man is an example of bearing "up under anything and everything"! Some of the last words Sha'ul wrote were to his spiritual son, Timothy:

"For I am already being poured out, and the time of my departure has arrived. I have fought the good fight, I have finished the race, I have guarded the belief. For the rest, there is laid up for me the crown of righteousness, which the Master, the righteous Judge, shall give to me on that Day, and not to me only but also to ALL THOSE LOVING HIS APPEARING." (2Tim 4:6-8, emphasis mine)

Am I a "cry-baby, pee-pee pants," whining and whimpering at the first sign of hardship? Do I turn tail and run, back-pedaling from the road block that stands in my way? Do I lay docile and impotent under attack, reluctant to "fight the good fight"? Am I unwilling to commit to a relationship because I sense it might demand more of me than I think I should have to give? Have I damaged a relationship with another because of my reluctance to commit? Do I need to restore this relationship to the best of my ability?

With Rav Sha'ul as our example, there is much that we can learn, and *do*...

"Brothers, I do not count myself to have reached the goal, but one thing I do, forgetting the things behind, and stretching forward to those things before, I PRESS TOWARD THE GOAL to receive the prize of victory of the highest calling of YAHWEH in Messiah Yahshua." (Phi 3:13-15 CJB, emphasis mine)

"And this I pray, that your love might extend more and more in knowledge and all discernment, for you to examine the matters that differ, in order to be sincere, and not stumbling, until the day of Messiah, being filled with the fruit of righteousness, through יהושע [Yeshua] Messiah, to the esteem and praise of Elohim." (Phi 1:9-11)

Notes:

_____

_____

_____

_____

_____

_____

_____

_____

_____

_____

_____

_____

_____

_____

_____

Elul 16

The Best

"Love ... is ever ready to believe the BEST of every person ... " (1Cor 13:7 AMPC, emphasis mine)

Noah Webster defines a "gossip" as "one who runs from house to house, tattling and telling news; an idle tattler."[10] A very dangerous practice, as often what is told is the *amended* truth, and this "new" version may destroy many lives in the retelling. Ancient Jewish wisdom condemns this practice of gossip, known as *LaSon Hara*, even to the one who listens, for it is criticizing and maligning one that is made in the image of our Creator.

When we walk in the love of YHWH our Elohim, we must *choose*, by a deliberate act of our will, to not listen to, or accept, the negative reports concerning other people. Instead, we must choose to believe in the deliverance of our Messiah Yeshua, knowing that He is "not desiring the destruction of any, but that all may be turned from their evil ways." (2Pet 3:9 BBE) Our Elohim is the God of the impossible (Luke 1:37). The day we fail to believe in this, and begin to believe the worst of every person, even our *own* redemption is suspect...

Am I willing to listen to *anything* anyone is telling me? Have I neglected the selective hearing that my Father requires of me? Have I willfully shared something that was told to me in confidence? Have I been quick to put forth an opinion concerning someone—whether true or not—that would have caused that person harm? Am I so "high minded" that I believe myself to be above this sin of *LaShon Hara*? Is there one that I have injured with the words of my mouth, and am I willing to humble myself, and seek restoration?

"YHWH, who shall sojourn in Your tabernacle? Who shall dwell upon Your set-

---

[10] ibid

apart mountain? He that walks uprightly, and works righteousness, and speaks truth in his heart; that has NO SLANDER upon his tongue, nor does no evil to his fellow, nor takes up a reproach against his neighbor; in whose eyes a vile person is despised, but he honors them that fear YHWH; he that swears to his own hurt, and changes not; he that puts not out his money on interest, nor takes a bribe against the innocent. He that does these things shall never be moved." (Ps 15 HRVS, emphasis mine)

Notes:

_____

_____

_____

_____

_____

_____

_____

_____

_____

_____

_____

_____

_____

_____

_____

_____

_____

_____

_____

_____

Elul 17

Never Gives Up

"{LOVE'S} ... hopes are fadeless under all circumstances, and it endures everything [without weakening]." (1Cor 13:7 AMPC, insert mine)

Daniel Webster has an interesting definition for the word "hope": "A desire of some good, accompanied with at least a slight expectation of obtaining it, or A BELIEF THAT IT IS OBTAINABLE. Hope differs from wish and desire in this, that it implies some expectation of obtaining the good desired, or the possibility of possessing it. Hope therefore always gives pleasure or joy; whereas wish and desire may produce or be accompanied with pain and anxiety"[11] (emphasis mine). It is certainly worthwhile to examine just *what* we are hoping for.

We are to hope in our Elohim, who is the God of hope (see Rom 15:13), and hope in the continuation of our deliverance (see 2Cor 1:10). We have hope in our Messiah (Eph 1:12), and have hope in the inheritance He has called us to (Eph 1:18; Col 1:5). We have hope concerning our future—what we call eternal life—*if* we hold fast to our Elohim, and His Torah (Heb 3:6, 10:23). And what of those of us who are holding out hope for our healing, something else that has been promised to us (1Pet 2:24; Isa 53:5).

However, just as when a light fades away into darkness, have I allowed my hope to fade away as well? Have I picked up the plate titled "discouragement," and allowed it to bloat me to the extent that my hope has been consumed? Has my *emunah*—my faith and trust—grown so thin that it can no longer be stood upon?

In Genesis 22, we are given the account of Abraham's *greatest* test of faith: the command to offer up his promised and cherished son, Isaac, as a sacrifice to our Creator. Not only is Abraham's love for YHWH evident in his quick and

---

[11] ibid

attentive response ("Here I am," verse 1), but the Torah also bears witness of his love for Isaac ("Now take your son, Isaac, your only one whom you love," verse 2). There is no hesitation revealed to us by Abraham, no doubting, just a complete and total trust that the Elohim who had called him, was in control. Even as Abraham placed Isaac on the wood, and raised the knife to offer him to YHWH our Elohim, he never gave up, not understanding, but *knowing*, YAH was in command.

On this mountain called Moriah, YHWH provided Abraham a ram to be offered up in place of his son Isaac (Gen 22:13). In this city called Jerusalem, Abba Father also offered up *His* Son, to take our place, that we might never give up, and always have the hope of eternal life. It is in this same city, Jerusalem, where our Messiah King will return to set up His kingdom, and will rule for the Millennium (Zec 14:4; Rev 21:2-27).

Notes:

_____

_____

_____

_____

_____

_____

_____

_____

_____

_____

_____

_____

_____

_____

_____

_____

_____

_____

Elul 18

Never Fails

"Love never fails [never fades out or becomes obsolete or comes to an end]."
(1Cor 13:8 AMPC)

We are told by Rav Sha'ul that the love of our Elohim—which is an everlasting love (Jer 31:3)—has been poured into and out of our hearts by the Holy Breath of Elohim (Rom 5:5). And yet most of us, just by our mere "human-ness," do not appear to *know* how to walk *in* the love of our Creator, which is, as always, one step at a time. We need to recognize that love begins as a choice. We choose, as an act of our will, whether we will walk and live in love or whether we will not. In reality, love has nothing to do with whether other people love us or not. It has everything to do with *our* choices under any and all circumstances.

Noah Webster lists multiple definitions for the word "fail"; here are some of them: "To become deficient; to be insufficient; to cease to be abundant for supply; or to be entirely wanting; to decay; to decline; to sink; to be diminished; to desert; to disappoint; to cease or to neglect or omit to afford aid, supply or strength."[12] The failure to live our lives through the power of the love of our Creator is a fault that lies with US, with choices that *we* have made.

Has my "love meter" ceased to register, reflecting in how I interact with other people? Have I allowed it to turn itself inward, toward myself, instead of outward, toward the people that are part of my world? Have I failed in my desire to exhibit the love of my Elohim to those around me, revealing to them to whom I belong? Does my love run hot and cold, on again and off again? Have I loved my neighbor as myself?

Help me, Abba, to love as *You* love ...

---

[12] ibid

"By this we have known love, because He laid down His life for us. And we ought to lay down our lives for the brothers ... My little children, let us not love in word or in tongue, but in DEED and in TRUTH." (1John 3:16,18, emphasis mine)

"This is My command, that you love one another, as I have loved you. No one has greater love than this: that one should lay down his life for his friends." (John 15:12-13)

"A renewed command I give to you, that you love one another, as I have loved you, that you also love one another. By this shall all know that you are My taught ones, if you have love for one another." (John 13:34-35)

Notes:

_____

_____

_____

_____

_____

_____

_____

_____

_____

_____

_____

_____

_____

_____

_____

_____

_____

_____

Elul 19

The Wayside

"A sower went out to sow his seed. And as he sowed, some indeed fell by the wayside. And it was trodden down, and the birds of the heaven devoured it." (Luke 8:5)

"And this is the parable: The seed is the word of Elohim. And those by the wayside are the ones who hear, then the devil comes and takes away the word from their hearts, lest having believed, they should be saved." (Luke 8:11-12)

All of us have selective hearing; this is a fact of life. Truthfully, we hear what we want to hear, and many times that which we *should* be listening to, is going in one ear and out the other. It all involves training and discipline, teaching ourselves to discern those words we need to hear, and how to discard the garbage.

And it still all comes down to choice. We are the ones who make the decision as to what we are going to retain, and what we are going to reject. Our adversary is not able to *take* anything from us that we are not willing to *give* him. By the simple fact of this "seed" being by the wayside, it is obvious a choice was made to relegate it to a place of little importance.

"Wayside" is defined as "the side of the way; land immediately adjacent to a road, highway, path, etc.; roadside."[13] West of the Mississippi, we find the phrase "bar ditch," which is a shortened form of "borrow ditch," a term meaning to "borrow" the dirt from a ditch to fill in the crown of a road.[14] It is unfortunate that the bar ditch is where we find the garbage that people toss out of their vehicles while driving by, everything from bottles, cans, empty bags from fast food restaurants, to just about anything you can imagine. The

---

[13] http://www.dictionary.com/browse/wayside?s=t
[14] https://en.wikipedia.org/wiki/Bar_ditch

common denominator is that this is all considered refuse, and no longer wanted.

Is this how I have treated the "seed of Elohim," His Word? Have I allowed His Word to *fall* amongst the items of discard, of garbage? Have I deliberately tuned out the hearing of my Father's Word, because I no longer value it as something that is priceless? Have I relegated it to a place of little importance, no longer of use?

"I have treasured up Your word in my heart, That I might not sin against You." (Ps 119:11)

"And these Words which I am commanding you today shall be in your heart, and you shall impress them upon your children, and shall speak of them when you sit in your house, and when you walk by the way, and when you lie down, and when you rise up, and shall bind them as a sign on your hand, and they shall be as frontlets between your eyes. And you shall write them on the doorposts of your house and on your gates." (Deu 6:6-9)

Notes:

_____

_____

_____

_____

_____

_____

_____

_____

_____

_____

_____

_____

_____

Elul 20

On the Rock

"And others fell on rocky places, where they did not have much soil, and immediately they sprang up, because they had no depth of soil. But when the sun was up they were scorched, and because they had no root they withered." (Mat 13:5-6)

"And that sown on rocky places, this is he who hears the word and immediately receives it with joy, yet he has no root in himself, but is short-lived, and when pressure or persecution arises because of the word, immediately he stumbles." (Mat 13:20-21)

Many years ago, on a camping trip into the Wind River Mountains of Wyoming, I remember seeing a small pine tree growing in the middle of a solid rock face. It was with amazement that I speculated on this small tree. The pine seed must have found just enough soil in that one place to germinate, and perhaps there was also a crack in the rock right there at that one spot, allowing the roots to anchor it to the side of the rock face. We have made subsequent trips back to that same area through the years, and that tree is still there. However, it does not appear to have grown much in the twelve to fourteen years that I have been observing it.

The Wind Rivers are predominantly formed of granite, and granite is *hard*. Because of its toughness, granite has long been used as a construction material, and is still a favorite for modern kitchen counter tops. It would be impossible and fruitless to sprout seeds from the top of such a counter; there would have to be another medium, such as soil, involved.

Let us turn all of this inward. Has my heart become so hardened that the Word of my Elohim can no longer find a place to take root? Am I now so shallow, that there is no depth to who I am? Do I close myself off, choking the Word within me, when trials and pressures come upon me? Have the boulders in my life stunted the growth of the Word within me? Have all of the rocks in my field eradicated and destroyed the light inside of me?

"He again defines a certain day, 'Today,'" saying through Dawid so much later, as it has been said, "Today, if you hear His voice, do not harden your hearts.'" (Heb 4:7)

Notes:

_____

_____

_____

_____

_____

_____

_____

_____

_____

_____

_____

_____

_____

_____

_____

_____

_____

_____

_____

_____

_____

_____

_____

_____

_____

_____

Elul 21

Thorns

"And other fell among thorns, and the thorns grew up with it and choked it." (Luke 8:7)

"And that which fell among thorns are those who, when they have heard, go out and are choked with worries, and riches, and pleasures of life, and bring no fruit to perfection." (Luke 8:14)

I grow a vegetable garden every year. It is something I enjoy doing, and the rewards are healthy and beneficial as well. However, sowing my seeds among weeds, stickers, and thorns is pointless; my harvest would be next to nothing. Weeds and thorns can multiply rapidly, and if allowed to grow unhindered, will eventually take over an entire garden area. They must not only be destroyed, but completely removed, before a successful harvest can be assured.

Here in eastern Wyoming, we have a sticker known as a "puncture vine," or "goathead." It is vicious, and is almost impossible to get rid of. This puncture vine starts out as a beautiful, almost fern-like plant, with small white flowers. Those flowers eventually become the hard, many-pointed sticker, capable of causing much pain when stepped on. If not destroyed, they soon become a carpet of these little white flowers, turning into a tapestry of nothing but stickers.

And so it us with us, in the garden of our hearts and lives. Many are the sources of weeds, thorns, and stickers in this world around us, and all of them are extremely efficient at choking the "light of life" within us (see John 1:4). Nonetheless, it is our own individual responsibility to examine everything we find growing in our lives, observe whether it is beneficial, or detrimental, and act accordingly. Fall house-cleaning, folks!

Am I so consumed with worry that I have no room for *emunah*, trust and faith in my Creator? Are the thoughts of financial success and riches my primary motive in all that I do? Is the concern for fulfilling my own personal pleasures more important to me than being pure and holy in *His* eyes?

"For this is what יהוה [YHWH] said to the men of Yehudah and Yerushalayim, "Break up your tillable ground, and do not sow among thorns. Circumcise yourselves unto יהוה [YHWH], and take away the foreskins of your hearts, you men of Yehudah and inhabitants of Yerushalayim, lest My wrath come forth like fire and burn, with none to quench it, because of the evil of your deeds." (Jer 4:3-4)

Notes:

_____

_____

_____

_____

_____

_____

_____

_____

_____

_____

_____

_____

_____

_____

_____

_____

_____

_____

_____

_____

_____

Elul 22

Good Soil

"And other fell on the good soil, and grew up, and yielded a crop a hundredfold." (Luke 8:8)

"And that on the good soil are those who, having heard the word with a noble and good heart, retain it, and bear fruit with endurance." (Luke 8:15)

The soil in my greenhouse is very sandy, and does not make for growing healthy vegetables. I have raised beds inside of my greenhouse, and have been diligently working toward amending the natural soil to something that will produce the harvest that I desire. I have added a little of this, a little of that, and quite a bit of this other, and after five years, it is all looking pretty good. I am excited about this year's harvest, which will probably be the best one yet. It has, however, been a lot of work to get it where it is today.

This Torah walk is one of obedience. This is the first key ingredient that we must use to amend the hostile environment within us: the *yetzer hara*, the evil inclination. Another is our *emunah*, our total trust and belief in the One who created us, that with *His* hands upon the reins of our lives, we need never fear. Reading and studying the *Word* of our Elohim is also a vital ingredient, for we must *know* what we believe. Mix all of this together, and we will be well on the way to being "fertile soil."

Time for more penetrating questions, brethren. Is my heart, my life, a fertile ground for the seeds of Torah to bear fruit in? Do I not only *hear* the Word, but do I also willingly and joyfully *accept* it, and *act* accordingly? Am I striving with everything in me to retain this Word of *Life*? What kind of fruit am I producing, and does it line up with the list given to me in Galatians 5:22-23? Am I patient while my fruit is maturing, not willing that it be aborted prematurely?

"Who does go up into the mountain of יהוה [YHWH]? And who does stand in His set-apart place? He who has innocent hands and a clean heart, Who did not bring his life to naught, And did not swear deceivingly. He receives a blessing from יהוה [YHWH], And righteousness from the Elohim of his deliverance." (Ps 24:3-5)

Notes:

_____

_____

_____

_____

_____

_____

_____

_____

_____

_____

_____

_____

_____

_____

_____

_____

_____

_____

_____

_____

_____

_____

_____

Elul 23

To Obey

"And in your seed all the nations of the earth shall be blessed, BECAUSE you have OBEYED My voice." (Gen 22:18, emphasis mine)

When I read this passage of Scripture, the word "obeyed" always stands out to me. What did Abraham "obey"? He heard, then *obeyed*, the voice of his Elohim. It was when I began to take a serious look at this word "obey" I discovered something of interest. In the Hebrew language, the word that has been translated as "obey" is the same word that also means "hear" (Strong's #8085, shâma´), as we find in Deuteronomy 6:4:

"Hear, O Yisra'ĕl: יהוה our Elohim, יהוה is one!" ("Sh'ma, Yisra'el! YHWH Eloheinu, YHWH echad")

Noah Webster defines "obey" as the following: "to comply with the commands, orders or instructions of a superior, or with the requirements of law, moral, political or municipal; to do that which is commanded or required, or to forbear doing that which is prohibited."[15] It becomes apparent to us that there is a need for attentive listening. How do we know what these instructions are if we first do not *hear* them, or, as is often our case today, *read* them? I would also venture to suggest that there is a sequence: first, we focus our attention on, and *listen/read*; then we *do* according to what we have heard/read.

I perceive that we have an imbalance in this procedure today. People are either not listening with their complete attention, or they are not applying what they are hearing with a corresponding action. This equals *danger*. Our Father has given us many, many promises throughout His Word, but they are contingent on *our* obedience.

---

[15] American Dictionary of the English Language, Daniel Webster, 1828

Have I reached the place where I cultivate a "dull" hearing? Am I no longer willing to absorb and act upon what I hear and read? Has my *halachah*, my Torah walk, become strictly automation, never fulfilling with joy what my Creator has laid out before me?

"Guard, and OBEY all these words which I command you, that it might be well with you and your children after you forever, when you do what is good and right in the eyes of יהוה [YHWH] your Elohim." (Deu 12:28, emphasis mine)

Notes:

_____

_____

_____

_____

_____

_____

_____

_____

_____

_____

_____

_____

_____

_____

_____

_____

_____

_____

_____

Elul 24

Seasoned

"You are the salt of the earth, but if the salt becomes tasteless, how shall it be seasoned? For it is no longer of any use but to be thrown out and to be trodden down by men." (Mat 5:13)

Salt in the Middle East is in plentiful supply, and found in several different forms. The Dead Sea, in Israel, has one of the highest percentages of salt of any body of water on the face of this earth, and is more than 1300 feet below sea level. Much of the salt taken from the area surrounding the Dead Sea is not pure salt, having other minerals mixed in with it. When exposed to natural elements, the outer layers, or crusts, will lose their "saltiness," and need to be removed. This would expose the inner layers, the pure salt, which could then be used for seasoning and preserving. The outer layers were most often used as a road base in the time of Messiah Yeshua, so yes, the worthless salt was trodden down by men (see our opening verse).

Salt does not only strengthen the flavor of food, but it also functions as a preservative from decay and corruption. And again, salt is one of the symbols of YHWH's covenant with us, His chosen people (see Numbers 18:19), and the covenant of salt is an eternal covenant. When Messiah Yeshua informs us that we are the salt of the earth, He is instructing us to function in those same duties in the society that we live in, strengthening the flavor and preserving from corruption. And herein is the key of the covenant of salt:

"Have salt in yourselves, and be at peace among one another." (Mark 9:50, emphasis mine)

The covenant begins with us, and the salt needs to be applied to our own lives first. As we continue to walk in surrender to the work of the Spirit of YHWH within us, the salt will season us, bringing out the fullness of our flavor. It will also expose hypocrisy and impurities, and burn them out of us, preserving in us the pure Word of Truth. Then, and only then, will we have the seasoning effect that Elohim desires us to have on the world around us.

Is my seasoning now of no effect? Have I reached the place of being too salty with my words and actions? Or perhaps I no longer have sufficient salt of my own, and my impurities require additional salt?

"Let your speech at all times be gracious (pleasant and winsome), SEASONED [as it were] WITH SALT, [so that you may never be at a loss] to know how you ought to answer anyone [who puts a question to you]." (Col 4:6 AMPC, emphasis mine)

Notes:

_____

_____

_____

_____

_____

_____

_____

_____

_____

_____

_____

_____

_____

_____

_____

_____

_____

_____

_____

_____

Elul 25

By Example

"Practice what you have learned and received and heard and seen IN ME, and model YOUR way of living on it ..." (Phi 4:9 AMPC, emphasis mine)

The concept of having a role model, someone we can pattern our lives after, is a biblical principle. Actions have always spoken louder than words. Many a time it is the consistency of a person's *life*, and *lifestyle*, that has won that "one person" over to the camp of YHWH, he (or she) who otherwise would not have been won.

Daniel was such a role model. The Bible speaks of Daniel having an "excellent spirit" (Dan 5:12,14; 6:3), and that no fault could be found in him (Dan 6:4). He is one of many examples that can be taken from the Word of our Elohim to pattern our lives after. The faith chapter, found in Hebrews 11, is a roll call of those that have gone before us, leaving us their examples to follow.

However, there are others still alive today that are worthy to be called role models. Look carefully at those that have been walking faithfully with our Creator for an extended period of time, and inspect the fruit that is visible in their lives. We can learn much from examples that are still before us if we would just watch, and listen... and then practice what we have "learned and received." And then "the God of peace (of untroubled, undisturbed well-being) will be with you." (Phi 4:9 Amp).

What kind of an example am I setting, in the way I live my life? How I treat others? In the things that I say? Am I the best ambassador of my Father's kingdom that I can possibly be? Are there still things in my life that I would not want other people to be doing? Or saying?

"Example is a lesson that all men can read."

GILBERT WEST

"For you yourselves know how you ought to IMITATE US, for we were not disorderly among you, nor did we eat anyone's bread without paying for it, but worked with labour and toil night and day, in order not to burden any of you, not because we do not have authority, but to make ourselves an EXAMPLE, for you to IMITATE US." (2The 3:7-9, emphasis mine)

Notes:

_____

_____

_____

_____

_____

_____

_____

_____

_____

_____

_____

_____

_____

_____

_____

_____

_____

_____

_____

_____

_____

_____

Elul 26

Fear of YHWH

"The fear of יהוה *[YHWH] is the beginning of wisdom, And the knowledge of the Set-apart One is understanding."* (Pro 9:10)

The following is listed in Noah Webster's dictionary as one of the definitions of "fear": "In scripture, fear is used to express a filial {as a child to a parent} passion. In good men, the fear of God is a holy awe or reverence of God and his laws, which springs from a just view and real love of the divine character, leading the subjects of it to hate and shun EVERY thing that can offend such a holy being, and inclining them to aim at perfect obedience."[16]

There is a simpler way of explaining this. *Because* of my love and devotion to my Creator, my Father, I never wish to be in the place or position of disappointing Him in His expectations of me. Neither do I ever want to find myself separated from my Elohim by a consequence of my own actions. Therefore, I strive to stay as close to my Abba as possible. I have, in the past, used the example of sticking to my Elohim with the force of Gorilla Glue, or even Permabond. And the only way this is possible is through obedience to *His* Word.

And yet, what has happened to the fear of YHWH in our present day and age? There is less and less of this fear evident, less reverence[17], and yes, even less respect for the holy, set-apart things of our Creator. *Why?*

Where is *my* fear of YHWH? Have I misplaced it, ignored it, ceased to treat it with any significance? Have I allowed an attitude of nonchalance, casual flippancy, to creep into my relationship with the *King* of Kings?

Most holy, *kadosh*, Father, I repent of a cheap and frivolous attitude toward

---

16 Ibid, insert and emphasis mine
17 Reverence is defined as fear mixed with respect, affection, esteem, and awe

You, my Creator. Unite my heart, YAH, to fear Your *holy* Name, to revere it, to hold You and all You stand for in the highest esteem. Train me, Master, to be of one mind and one heart, undivided in the reverential and respectful fear of You. Thank You, Abba, that as I continue to walk in this healthy fear of You, You will continue to fill me with all of the godly knowledge, instruction, and wisdom that I need to walk my everyday life. In the Name, and in the authority of, Yeshua of Nazareth, and all that He represents, I pray... AMEIN!

"The reverent fear and worship of the Lord is the beginning of Wisdom and skill [the preceding and the first essential, the prerequisite and the alphabet]; a good understanding, wisdom, and meaning have all those who do [the will of the Lord]. Their praise of Him endures forever." (Ps 111:10 AMPC)

Notes:

_____

_____

_____

_____

_____

_____

_____

_____

_____

_____

_____

_____

_____

_____

_____

_____

_____

_____

Elul 27

Forgiveness

"Who is a God like You, Who forgives iniquity and passes over the transgression of the remnant of His heritage? He retains not His anger forever, because He delights in mercy and loving-kindness. He will again have compassion on us; He will subdue and tread underfoot our iniquities. You will cast all our sins into the depths of the sea." (Mic 7:18-19 AMPC)

The mother of my first husband was a very bitter, vindictive, unforgiving woman. The first time I met my future in-laws, they had not spoken to each other in over a year, all the while residing within the same house. This sad state of affairs was all because the husband had said (or done) something that had made the wife angry. And from what I learned, this was not the first time she had imposed this type of punishment on her husband. When my then mother-in-law died, some years later, she had already been confined to a wheel chair for several years, due mostly to complications from arthritis. Yet the things she held close to her heart were the many grudges she held against people that had "done her wrong," and she took these grudges to her grave.

Unforgiveness and bitterness are a cancer that will eat you alive, both physically and spiritually. You see, brethren, when it comes right down to "where the rubber meets the road," unforgiveness has its root in pride, and this is something YHWH cannot tolerate in His kingdom. When we choose *not* to forgive an offense, a wrong done, a hurt suffered, we set ourselves up as judge, jury, and executioner of the one that did the wrong to us, and that is a position reserved for our Elohim. Basically, we are pushing YHWH off of His throne, saying "I will handle *this* one…"

Has anyone done something to me as horrible as what people have done to the Father, in that they slaughtered and executed Yeshua, the perfect Son of Elohim? Am I not continually rejecting the Father's love and care? Yet *Elohim Avinu*, God our Father, chooses to forgive. Am I so much *better* and *bigger* than my Abba Father, that I cannot (or will not) forgive another that is made in *His* image? And is there someone to whom I must go, and offer them the forgiveness that the Father requires me to give?

Our Father knows the bondage of unforgiveness; it is one of the reasons for our Messiah's death, to free us from this bondage. But the key to receiving our own forgiveness from Father God is to *first* forgive others (see Mat 6:14-14). Once we choose to release forgiveness, then we have first and foremost restored our relationship with the Father. As we persevere in this forgiveness—and it may not be easy—it will allow Elohim to act in our behalf, because now our heart is in right relationship with *Him*. In this case, I know what I am talking about: I had to learn to walk in forgiveness with this mother-in-law, and her son, the one that I was married to. My first husband was extremely abusive, even tried to kill me several times, but my Abba was faithful, and delivered me out of the lion's mouth. But I *had* to walk in forgiveness before He did so...

"Be gentle and forbearing with one another and, if one has a difference (a grievance or complaint) against another, readily pardoning each other; even as the Lord has [freely] forgiven you, so MUST you also [forgive]." (Col 3:13 AMPC, emphasis mine)

Notes:

_____

_____

_____

_____

_____

_____

_____

_____

_____

_____

_____

_____

Elul 28

Integrity

"Judge me, O יהוה, [YHWH] according to my righteousness, And according to my integrity within me." (Ps 7:8)

One of the definitions of "integrity," according to the dictionary, is "the quality or state of being of sound moral principle; uprightness, honesty, and sincerity."[18] Basically, in common sense language, integrity means *doing what is right when no one is around to watch, because it is the right thing to do.* It does not necessarily mean perfection, but it does mean striving, trying, and setting a standard for yourself that you refuse to compromise on.

David was a person who lived a life of integrity, even before he became king. While being hunted down and driven from town to town, David had several opportunities to take matters into his own hands, and get even with the one hunting him. King Saul's desire was to see David dead, and when circumstances put Saul into David's hands, integrity would not allow David to harm "the anointed of the Lord" (1Sam 24:6). Saul recognized David's righteous and honorable character (1Sam 24:17-19), as did YHWH Elohim.

What are *my* plans and *my* actions, when I think no one is watching, when I think no one can trace "things" back to me? Are the plans and actions I engage in able to stand under the microscope of the purifying agent of Elohim's Torah, His Word? Are the intents and motives of *my* life, *my* heart, as transparent and pure before YHWH as I think they are?

"The integrity of the upright shall guide them, but the willful contrariness and crookedness of the treacherous shall destroy them." (Pro 11:3 AMPC)

Brethren, our Master Yeshua plainly told us that we are "the light of the

---

[18] Webster's New World Dictionary, 3rd College Edition, 1991

world" and a city set on a hill (Mat 5:14). In other words, everyone is watching us. Everything we do and say must be done with an attitude of integrity, with uprightness, with sound moral principle, as ambassadors of our Messiah King. And He *will* reward us accordingly…

"Those who sow righteousness gain a true reward." (Pro 11:18 CJB)

Notes:

_____

_____

_____

_____

_____

_____

_____

_____

_____

_____

_____

_____

_____

_____

_____

_____

_____

_____

_____

_____

_____

_____

Elul 29

A Day of Repentance

"Therefore say to the house of Yisra'ĕl, 'Thus said the Master יהוה [YHWH], "Repent, and turn back from your idols, and turn back your faces from all your abominations."'" (Eze 14:6, emphasis mine)

Tonight, at sundown, marks the beginning of the Hebrew month of Tishri. This date is also the *first* of the fall feasts of our Elohim (see Leviticus 23), known to many as *Yom Teruah*, the Feast of Trumpets, and also called *Rosh Hashanah*. According to the Hebrew calendar, this is the beginning of the civil New Year, and ancient Jewish wisdom believes that this is also the day that YHWH created Adam and *Chavah*, commonly known as Eve. If we would have been following the "appointed times," we would have spent this last month of Elul as a time of self-examination and *teshuvah* (repentance) before our Creator, confessing our sins, transgressions, and shortcomings. Repentance is *the* key to entering into the coming New Year, walking in the covenant of His blessings for the entire year.

True repentance is *not* feeling guilt from getting caught when we were doing something wrong. According to Noah Webster, repentance is "sorrow or deep contrition for sin, as AN OFFENSE AND DISHONOR TO GOD, a violation of His holy law, and the basest ingratitude towards a Being of infinite benevolence. This is called evangelical repentance, and is accompanied and followed by amendment {change for the better} of life."[19] There is an *anguish*, a pain, and a sense of trust being broken on the part of the one committing the sin. True repentance will *always* accept personal responsibility for the sin and wrong-doing that was done, and will consequently turn away from the behavior that caused the sin problem in the first place. This is *teshuvah*—turning away from evil, and turning *back* to YHWH.

---

[19] Ibid; insert and emphasis mine

Messiah Yeshua made a way for us to come to the Throne of Grace, to cleanse our hearts in repentance, and to obtain mercy in our time of need (Hebrews 4:16). Yeshua is the "Mercy Seat" we run to, where we find forgiveness for our sins on a daily basis (1John 1:9), and not just once a year. During this time of *Yom Teruah*, let us make an effort to examine ourselves (2Cor 13:5, 1Cor 11:28), for our YHWH Elohim is looking, looking, running to and fro...

"For the eyes of יהוה [YHWH] diligently search throughout all the earth, to show Himself strong on behalf of those whose heart IS PERFECT TO HIM." (2Chr 16:9, emphasis mine)

"I advise you to buy from Me gold refined in the fire, so that you become rich; and white garments, so that you become dressed, so that the shame of your nakedness might not be shown; and anoint your eyes with ointment, so that you see. As many as I love, I reprove and discipline. So be ardent and REPENT." (Rev 3:18-19, emphasis mine)

Notes:

_____

_____

_____

_____

_____

_____

_____

_____

_____

_____

_____

_____

_____

_____

Tishri 1

Hate

"These six matters יהוה [YHWH] hates ... " (Pro 6:16)

As a young child, my Danish mother would reprimand me severely for using the word "hate" concerning anything—from different foods, or the weather, or even concerning people who would irritate me. Mom believed that this word was all but a cussword (oh, horrors!), and with the English vocabulary being as extensive as it is, there was *surely* a more appropriate word to describe my feelings. To this day, I still hesitate when I use the word "hate," just because of the lesson instilled in me from my mother.

To say that our Creator "hates" something—in this case, there are six "somethings"—it must be very strong indeed. The Hebrew word used here is the word *śânê'* (Strong's H8130), and is only used one hundred forty-six times in the entire Tanakh (the Old Testament), with a mere fourteen times in the Torah. Jeff Benner defines *śânê'* as "intense hostility and aversion, usually deriving from fear, anger, or sense of injury; extreme dislike or antipathy."[20] For our Elohim to even possess this type of feeling is so opposite of what the westernized Christian Church teaches, that perhaps it is past time for us to sit up and pay attention, and discover the *why* behind this statement.

Are there things, people, and matters, that I have an intense hostility and aversion toward? Is this the correct attitude for me to have concerning these matters? Perhaps I need to look more closely at why I have these feelings of extreme dislike, and see if the problem isn't within *me*.

"Do not hate your brother in your heart. Reprove your neighbour, for certain, and bear no sin because of him." (Lev 19:17)

---

[20] Ancient Hebrew Dictionary, Jeff Benner, ©2007

Notes:

Tishri 2

Abomination

"And seven are an abomination to Him ..." (Pro 6:16)

The Hebrew word that is translated as "abomination" is the word *tô'ēbah* (Strong's H8441), and literally means something that is disgusting and loathsome. The distinguished gentleman of yesteryear, Noah Webster, defines "abomination" as following: "1. Extreme hatred; detestation; 2. The object of detestation; 3. Hence, defilement, pollution, in a physical sense, or evil doctrines and practices, which are moral defilements, idols and idolatry, are called abominations. The Jews were an abomination to the Egyptians; and the sacred animals of the Egyptians were an abomination to the Jews. In short, whatever is an object of extreme hatred, is called an abomination."[21] It appears that our Elohim has moved past the place of intense aversion and hostility to outright disgust and extreme hatred.

It would be common sense for me to realize that I do *not* want to be on the receiving end of YHWH's disgust and extreme hatred. Perhaps I need to ask myself: are there parts of Torah that I have been deliberately ignoring, choosing to believe that they do not pertain to me? Have I been treating the words of Torah as if they were green bologna, instead of the prime rib that they are? Have I allowed myself to become that object of disgust in my Father's eyes?

Father, my Father, help me to become that child of the *El Elyon*, the *Most* high Elohim, that I desire to be. Abba, I want to sit at Your feet, and feed from Your Word, always learning and digesting that which You teach me. Help me to hold fast to the Word of *Life*, never turning it loose. Help me to be pleasing in *Your* sight... In Yeshua's Name, Amein.

---

21 American Dictionary of the English Language, Noah Webster, 1828

Notes:

Tishri 3

Pride

"A proud look ... " (Pro 6:17)

The Hebrew word that has been translated here as "proud" is the word *rûm* (Strong's H7311), and carries with it the sense of some *one*, or some *thing*, that is lifted up, exalted, raised up, and magnified. Many Bible versions have translated this word as "haughty," or "arrogant"; both words would be appropriate.

Throughout the Torah, *rûm* is used in conjunction with the idea of lifting up offerings to our Creator, a positive thing. However, I found a verse in Deuteronomy 17 that speaks of the heart of the king being "lifted up" above his brethren, exalting himself above all others, a bad thing (verse 20, see also Deu 8:11-14). It would appear that when one's heart becomes lifted up through self-exaltation, one tends to forget the ways and the Word of our Elohim.

Rûm is the opposite of humility, the one who is of a humble and contrite spirit, the one that our Elohim is pleased to dwell with (see Isa 57:15). Repeatedly, throughout the Word of our Elohim, we are told that YWHW resists the proud (Jam 4:6), rebukes them (Ps 119:21), and will not put up with them (Ps 101:5). The way of the proud is considered a sin (Pro 21:4), yet all too often, we find ourselves walking in that way. Why? Again, we deal with the *yetzer hara*, the evil inclination, that does not consider anything as wrong, or sinful.

How much pride is found in *me*? Do I do and say things out of a proud and arrogant nature? Do I exhibit a spirit of pride in my "humility," as in "Look at me! See how humble I am"? Do I truly consider myself above everyone else? Am I willing to wash the sores of the filthiest leper, simply because my Master was willing to die for such a one, or am I just too "good" to dirty my hands with such a mundane task?

"Everyone proud in heart is an abomination to יהוה [YHWH]; Hand to hand: he goes not unpunished ... Before destruction comes pride, And before a fall a haughty spirit! Better to be lowly in spirit with the poor, Than to divide the spoil with the proud." (Pro 16:5; 18-19)

Notes:

_____

_____

_____

_____

_____

_____

_____

_____

_____

_____

_____

_____

_____

_____

_____

_____

_____

_____

_____

_____

_____

_____

_____

Tishri 4

Deception

"A lying tongue ... " (Pro 6:17)

All too often, we find the one who walks in his/her own self-importance resorting to deception and fabrication in order to maintain the façade of arrogance and pride that they have established. Plainly speaking, these are the ones who "tell stories" to confirm they are all that they say they are, when in reality, they are not. I believe our friend, Noah Webster, defines this as "hypocrisy": "simulation; a feigning to be what one is not; or dissimulation, a concealment of one's real character or motives. More generally, hypocrisy is simulation, or the assuming of a false appearance of virtue or religion; a deceitful show of a good character, in morals or religion".[22]

The story that is related to us in Acts 5 exemplifies the depths of Elohim's hatred for those who lie, especially to *Him*. We have the illustration of a couple who walked in their own self-importance, boasting of selling property and turning the proceeds over to the Messianic community at Jerusalem. Their hypocrisy lay in the fact that they had *not* turned loose of all of the money. Not trusting the Creator of the universe to meet all of their needs, they kept back a portion of the sale money for themselves. A costly deception for them.

It seems to be inherent in human nature to want others to think well of us. However, when we resort to deception to portray an admirable image, we are aligning ourselves with our adversary, the father of *all* lies (see John 8:44). It is only when we learn to accept the truth of who and what we are, that we will no longer need to promote this false image of what we are not. We *are* children of *the* King, we walk in right relationship with our Creator, and we are accepted in the beloved (Eph 1:5-6).

---

[22] ibid

Is this deception something I practice habitually? Do I deliberately tell untruths, in order that I might elevate myself? Do I fabricate situations and events to make myself look better and bigger? Is there anyone that I need to "spill the beans" to, admit my deceptions, and ask for forgiveness?

"יהוה [YHWH] who does sojourn in Your Tent? Who does dwell in Your set-apart mountain? He who walks blamelessly, And does righteousness, And speaks the truth in his heart." (Ps 15:1-2)

Notes:

_____

_____

_____

_____

_____

_____

_____

_____

_____

_____

_____

_____

_____

_____

_____

_____

_____

_____

_____

_____

_____

Tishri 5

Shredding

"And hands shedding innocent blood ... " (Pro 6:17)

We *do* things with our hands; our hands will invariably give action to the thoughts and intents of the heart (see 1Chr 29:18). Therefore, if our hearts and our eyes are filled with arrogance and pride, if our mouths speak only those things that solidify our conceit, it bears speculation as to what our hands might be doing.

What happens when a congregation splits? All too often the cause of such a split is the arrogance of a group of individuals who are certain that *they* are in the right, while everyone else is in the wrong. Unwilling to humble themselves and *bend*—please note that I did not say compromise, I said bend—these people leave behind a fractured and wounded assembly, many of them not even involved in the issue that caused the split. And what of those who are new to this Torah walk? Where does this type of action leave them? We have all, I am relatively sure, heard the phrase "Don't shoot the wounded."

How can I turn this inward, looking at myself? Have I, in my desire to satisfy my own self-esteem, shredded the lives of those who are innocent of any wrong doing? Like a pebble in a pond, have I closely looked at the effect on others the work of my hands might have? Is the work of my hands committed to the honor of the One who made them? Is there anyone to whom I need to seek forgiveness from?

"In the transgression of the lips is an evil snare, But the righteous gets out of distress. From the fruit of his mouth one is filled with good, And the work of a man's hands is given back to him." (Pro 12:13-14)

"And to make it your ambition to live peaceably, and to attend to your own, and to work with your own hands, as we commanded you, so that you behave decently toward those who are outside, and not be in any need." (1The 4:11-12)

Notes:

Tishri 6

Wickedness

"A heart devising wicked schemes ..." (Pro 6:18)

So often, we hear the phrase "the Father knows my heart," and this is entirely true; however, do *we* know our own heart? The Word of our Elohim tells us that "the heart is deceitful above all things, and desperately wicked: who can know it?" (Jer 17:9 KJV) which, when you combine it with the *yetzer hara*, the evil inclination, is a recipe for disaster.

Laban, the father-in-law of Jacob, was such a one who "devised wicked schemes." Being fully aware of the blessings of Elohim that covered Jacob, Laban schemed concerning the bride-price of not just one wife, but two, and always to his own advantage (see Gen 29). And again, concerning the division of all the livestock, Laban devised a scheme that for all intents and purposes, should have been totally in his favor. None of Laban's schemes came to fruition, however, and Jacob left Laban a prosperous man (see Gen 30:25-43). As it is written, "Many are the plans in a man's heart, but it is the counsel of יהוה [YHWH] that stands." (Pro 19:21)

It is easy, way too easy, when we find ourselves victims of slander, for example, to think and meditate on ways to "get even." Another instance to examine is our reaction when someone causes pain to those we love. Because of the deceitfulness of our own hearts, we have the potential of coming up with some serious methods of retribution, which, if we ever acted upon them, would nullify our confession of faith.

Messiah Yeshua told us that it is out of the overflow of the heart a person's mouth speaks (Luke 6:45). Are the words of my mouth revealing hidden wickedness and evil within my heart? Do I ponder on ways to do injury to others? Have I set myself up as judge, jury, and executioner within those secret places of my heart?

Abba, Father, help me. Your word tells me that only those who are pure in heart shall ever see You, and I cannot but recognize the ugliness that is still within me. Create in me that *clean* heart, my Elohim, and renew that *right* spirit within me. In the Name of, and in the authority of, my Messiah Yeshua I pray...

Notes:

_____

_____

_____

_____

_____

_____

_____

_____

_____

_____

_____

_____

_____

_____

_____

_____

_____

_____

_____

_____

_____

_____

Tishri 7

Halacha

"Feet quick to run to evil..." (Pro 6:18)

The Hebrew word *halacha* means literally to go, or to walk, and refers to the *how* in which we choose to walk out our lives.[23] In all areas of our lives, we are to be guided and led by the Word of Elohim, in particular, His Torah, and as such, we then become "a letter of Messiah," read by all men (2Cor 3:2-3).

But what happens when our *halacha* is no longer one of consistent commitment and obedience? What happens when our walk ventures into areas of compromise—what kind of a message is this sending to those who are watching?

The story of Samson is one many of us can remember from our youth—days spent in "Children's Church." Yet much of what we were taught is *not* the whole story. We know that Samson was called to be a Nazarite from before his birth, but how many truly understand the significance of what the vow of a Nazarite really meant! It is not *just* abstaining from everything derived from grapes, and it is not *just* about letting their hair grow. It is a total dedication and consecration to the God of Abraham, Isaac, and Jacob.

Scripture records for us that Samson did not take the vow of the Nazarite seriously: he married a woman from one of the forbidden tribes, he frequently drank wine, it did not bother him to touch a dead corpse, and he was flippant about the source of his great strength (Jud 14-16). His life failed to be one of consistent commitment and obedience, and it cost him dearly.

Please note that I have used the word "consistent" accompanying the words commitment and obedience. We have all made mistakes that we have instantly

---

[23] http://www.myjewishlearning.com/article/halakhah-the-laws-of-jewish-life/

regretted. Nevertheless, when we are consistent in our desire to be committed and obedient, we will never deliberately and wantonly *run* to do evil—it is no longer part of our character.

Yet there are still times like this, when we need to stop and inspect ourselves, looking always for those areas where there could be room for improvement. Where have I compromised the standards set for me within the pages of Torah? Is my obedience instantaneous, or with reluctance? Is my walk all that I think it is, or do I spend more time stubbing my toes than actually walking?

Notes:

_____

_____

_____

_____

_____

_____

_____

_____

_____

_____

_____

_____

_____

_____

_____

_____

_____

_____

_____

_____

_____

Tishri 8

The Witness

"A false witness breathing out lies ... " (Pro 6:19)

Torah is adamant concerning the need for a minimum of two witnesses of every allegation of wrong doing; there is no such thing as circumstantial evidence found within the pages of Torah. Should someone bring an accusation against an individual, and the accusation proves to be false, then the one who first made the false accusation will receive the punishment reserved for the person that had been originally accused (see Deu 19:15-20). The commandment concerning bearing false witness is part of the Ten Words, also known as the Ten Commandments (Ex 20:16, Deu 5:20), and is a serious offence.

It is unfortunate that in our day and age, much circumstantial evidence has put innocent people behind bars, sometimes for life. We perceive this and that is so, but we really do not know if it is or not. We have not actually *seen* with our eyes, or *heard* with our ears, and yet many times we condemn the innocent with little factual information. All too often, opinions are given as facts, when they are not. Noah Webster defines this as "perjury"—"The act or crime of willfully making a false oath, when lawfully administered"[24]—yet the consequences of this act no longer seem to be as serious.

Scripture records for us that it was with false witnesses that our Messiah was convicted and sentenced to death (Mat 26:59, Mark 14:55-56), violating the very Torah that the priesthood was supposed to be guarding. We know and understand the death of our Messiah was the will of Elohim. Be that as it may, it is not difficult to speculate what the eventual end of those who gave their false testimony would have been.

---

[24] ibid

Am I also guilty? Have I condemned others only on hearsay, without seeing or hearing the supposed wrong that was done? Have I been all too quick to believe the worst without first examining the facts, and researching whatever documentation was available? Have I willingly given a false report, whether to the good or the bad, of someone or something, that I should not have done? Are there ones, made in the image of our Elohim, that I need to seek forgiveness from, for speaking an untruth about?

"Take this Book of the Torah, and you shall place it beside the ark of the covenant of יהוה [YHWH] your Elohim, and it shall be there as a witness against you ... " (Deu 31:26)

"I have called the heavens and the earth as witnesses today against you: I have set before you life and death, the blessing and the curse. Therefore you shall choose life, so that you live, both you and your seed, to love יהוה [YHWH] your Elohim, to obey His voice, and to cling to Him – for He is your life and the length of your days ... " (Deu 30:19-20) **Notes:**

_____

_____

_____

_____

_____

_____

_____

_____

_____

_____

_____

_____

_____

_____

_____

_____

Tishri 9

Strife

"And one who causes strife among brothers." (Pro 6:19)

Many Bible versions use the word "discord" in this verse. The actual Hebrew word is *medân* (Strong's H4090), and means strife, discord, and contention. It is interesting to note that this particular word is only used three times in the Tanakh—the Old Testament—and all are found within the book of Proverbs, concerning relationships between people.

What are the causes of strife? Turning again to Mr. Webster, he defines strife as "1. Exertion or contention for superiority; contest of emulation, either by intellectual or physical efforts. 2. Contention in anger or enmity; contest; struggle for victory; quarrel or war. 3. Opposition; contrariety; contrast."[25] By looking at this definition, I suggest to you that *all* of the previous six attributes that our Elohim hates will lead to strife among the brethren.

Torah is all about community and relationships, about how we deal with one another, and how we interact with our Elohim. Messiah Yeshua tells us that the two greatest commandments are first, to love our Creator with everything in us, and second, to love our neighbor as we love and care for ourselves (Luke 10:25-28). With this being the case, it is not difficult to understand why this seventh "matter," the causing of strife, is such an abomination, such a thing of contempt and disgust, to the One who formed us.

We are all individuals, with our personal likes and dislikes. Occasionally, there will be that one who will rub us the wrong way, and whom we have a difficult time getting along with. This is human nature; our Father never desired a race of identical clones. Despite all of this, we must remember that there is no ceiling on good manners, and the fruit that we display (Gal 5:22-23) are there to

---

[25] ibid

be tested by those around us.

Have I caused strife and division among those that are called by *His* name, and is this something that I take pleasure in doing? Am I rude and ungrateful, refusing to give my brothers and sisters sufficient room to make, and learn, from their own mistakes? Am I so self-righteous that I no longer care who I offend? Are the Fruit of the Spirit that are trying to mature in my life falling to the ground, aborted and green?

Father, my Father, forgive me. Forgive me for being so absorbed in myself, that I neglected to consider those whom You have placed in my world. Forgive me for all of the seeds of strife, discontent, and discord that I have sown, and help me, Abba, to always place the needs of others before myself. Help me to honor and respect those who are created in *Your* image, and to always treat them with dignity. Amein.

Notes:

_____

_____

_____

_____

_____

_____

_____

_____

_____

_____

_____

_____

_____

_____

_____

Tishri 10

Fruit of Repentance

"Produce the fruit of perfect repentance." (Mat 3:8 Hebrew Gospel of Matthew, George Howard, ©1995)

According to the forces of nature, we know that apples produce apples, corn produces corn, and roses produce thorns, but eventually also roses, and some even produce "rose hips" as well. Elohim spoke it, decreed it, and every seed produces after its own kind (Gen 1:11). "Fruit," according to the dictionary, can also mean the "production, effect or consequence" of an action or event[26].

Let us therefore look at the action of "perfect repentance." First, repentance is *not* remorse: simply being sorry we got caught doing wrong, with the accompanying fear of discipline and punishment. Repentance is the gut-wrenching, heart-breaking, deeply felt sorrow that we experience, knowing that we have offended and dishonored our Creator and Father. With this sorrow is the recognition of the need to *change*. Whatever the course of action was that led us to the place where we violated our Elohim's Word and Covenant, whatever it was that brought us to the instant where we *knew* we needed to repent, the fact remains that a change is required.

This change in our actions, our lifestyle, is the "fruit of perfect repentance." When we make a deliberate decision, an act of our own choice, to no longer *do* the things that are in direct violation and opposition to the Word of Elohim, we are producing the correct fruit. We are choosing to allow the *Ruach HaKodesh*, the Spirit of Elohim, to have His way within us, and to allow the Fruit of YHWH to mature in us as well (see Gal 5:22-26). And this is how the world will know to *Whom* we belong...

"You did not choose Me, but I chose you and appointed you that you should

---

[26] ibid

go and bear fruit, and that your fruit should remain, so that whatever you ask the Father in My Name He might give you." (John 15:16)

"Repent therefore, and be restored so that your sins be blotted out and times of rest come to you from the presence of YHWH, and He send to you Him who was prepared for you, Yeshua the Messiah ..." (Acts 3:19-20 HRVS)

Notes:

_____

_____

_____

_____

_____

_____

_____

_____

_____

_____

_____

_____

_____

_____

_____

_____

_____

_____

_____

SUMMATION

By Kathy Hamlett

"Let us hear the conclusion of the entire matter: Fear Elohim and guard His commands, for this applies to all mankind! For Elohim shall bring every work into right-ruling, including all that is hidden, whether good or whether evil." (Ecc 12:13-14)

As we have traveled the Days of Awe, reevaluating ourselves, let us hear the conclusion of the matter. With Elohim, who is the Ultimate Judge, all actions we have taken will end in a right ruling. This right ruling may work for us, but it may work against us. The choice has been ours and will continue to be ours until the day our spirit leaves this human body.

During these Days of Awe, we shed tears and did *teshuvah*, followed by *tikkun* (an act of restoration). We have sought out those we have come against to try and make amends with before our "gift" is acceptable to Elohim. The Ultimate Judge, Elohim, will weigh us in the scales of His justice. Our recourse during this time determines our continuance of justice. May we all be found worthy to be found in the Book of Life.

L'shanah tovah tikatev v'taihatem

May you be inscribed and sealed for a good year.

ABOUT THE AUTHOR

Mette Marx was born in the U.S. Virgin Islands, but the pathways of life led her through different countries of the world before settling her in the western United States. She first came to the high desert of Wyoming in the fall of 1973, and fell in love with the wide-open spaces—truly Elohim's country, "where the deer and the antelope play."

Mette's writing ability was, in part, inherited: both of her parents were writers, and encouraged her to join them in this adventure. Mette has understood that writing is a talent the Creator has deposited within her, and He will pull it out of her in His good timing. Mette also believes that Elohim is still refining and perfecting the writing she does.

Mette is married to the man that she believes "Elohim handpicked to join me to." They have a testimony of their adventure toward marriage, and beyond. Richard supports Mette in her writing, and is very much her other half, besides being her best friend.

Mette can be found on Facebook, where she not only has a personal profile, but also has a "fan page" under the title of "Bread from the Basket." Her devotionals are posted regularly, for all to read and enjoy.

Made in the USA
Columbia, SC
09 August 2017